Playing Basketball

An ARM CHAIR GUIDE

Full of 100 Tips to Getting Better at Basketball

Arm Chair Guides

Playing Basketball:
An Arm Chair Guide Full of 100 Tips to Getting Better at Basketball

Published by
Arm Chair Guides

Printed in the United States of America

ISBN-13: 978-0615502076
ISBN-10: 0615502075

Visit the Arm Chair Guides site at:
www.ArmChairGuides.com/PlayingBasketball

Overview

Basketball is one of those games in which natural talent helps tremendously in becoming a potential professional basketball player; however, it is not the only thing.

Every professional basketball player had to endure hours of practice in every fundamental of the game in order for the action to become automatic. The skills required for dribbling, passing and shooting have to be practiced and perfected in order to succeed in the sport.

Seeking to devise an indoor activity since the Massachusetts winters were bitterly cold, Dr. James Naismith used a soccer ball and two peach baskets as goals, which later developed into the "second fastest game in the world" after ice hockey. Basketball comprises of two teams of five players each with the goal of getting the ball across a rectangular court using combinations of dribbles, passes and sprinting to the opponent's side of the court. The ball is then shot into a basket elevated ten feet off the ground in order to score points.

The sport has gone through various modifications over the years, such as the court markings, rules, equipment and style of play. Understanding the basics can help you improve your game as a player or appreciate the game better as a spectator.

Arc your shot.

Every player has a different arc to their shot – some flat, some more curved. The trick is to have a medium arc that will "swish" into the basket. Too flat and the ball will bounce off of the rim. A shot with too much arc is usually inconsistent and hard to control.

Develop a good, technically sound method and stick to it every time.

This will give you more control as well as making you more consistent in your shooting when you make a free throw.

Do what the pros do.

Arguably one of the greatest basketball players, Michael Jordan use to "hang" in the air longer than his opponents, which enabled him to beat most of them. His shooting was independent of his jumping which made him even more of a shooting threat. Watch some of his videos and try to duplicate his style to make you a "shooting threat" as well.

Develop a proper shooting technique.

Use BEEF (Balance, Eye, Elbow, Follow-Through). Each of these elements are important, especially the follow-through. Remember, last contact with the ball will determine its flight path.

Relax and concentrate.

Aim at the back of the front rim toward the center of the basket. When shooting lay-ups or bank shots, aim at the point of the backboard where the shot would bank into the basket.

Take the good shot.

Players must find the right balance between shooting too often and not shooting enough. As players develop, they will learn how to determine what is a good shot to take.

Learn to balance.

When shooting, proper balance from side to side and front to back is necessary in order for the ball to follow the correct path into the basket. This takes time to develop.

Follow through on every shot.

Follow-through is important since the last contact with the ball determines its flight path. By holding this position for a split second more, you can also recognize your mistakes when shooting.

Don't force it.

The jump should be a natural jump, not a forced one. The ball should be released at the top of the jump, just before descending. A recommended technique to remember is 'up, hang, shoot'.

Keep it simple.

Players should be relaxed, focus on the basket and shoot with their knees slightly bent. Keeping their free-throw routine simple enables players to focus more on their shot rather than their routine. Excessive and unnecessary movements should be avoided, using only motions that are essential to the shot.

Try using the wall.

This is one of the best passing drills in perfecting accuracy and proficiency as well as getting warmed-up.

Paint or tape three X's on a solid wall at varying heights. Stand back ten feet and try hitting them in different order using different passes, such as the two-handed chest pass, the two-handed overhead pass and the two-handed bounce pass. After successfully hitting the targets ten times in a row, move back five feet and repeat until you reach twenty feet away.

Practice with others.

Form a triangle with three players at least ten feet apart. As quickly as you can, pass the ball to another player in random order using each of the different types of passes: the two-handed chest pass, the two-handed overhead pass and the two-handed bounce pass. You can make it fun by devising a "penalty" for a missed catch.

Recover your balance.

After receiving a bad pass, be sure to regain your balance before throwing another pass. A bad pass can usually lead to another bad pass.

Use a baseball pass to transport the ball down the court quickly.

As the name implies, the baseball pass is thrown overhand to a player sprinting up the court, over the defense. The hand must be behind the ball so that there is no spin to render it uncatchable.

Use the behind-the-back pass to deceive your opponent.

The behind-the-back pass is a relatively easy pass to learn. It's quite deceptive but should not be used to show off. Holding the ball in the dominant hand, the player just flicks the ball from behind his back to another player using wrist strength and flexibility.

Do a bounce pass when under defensive pressure.

The ball should bounce about 2/3 of the way from your waist to the receiver's waist. The ball is slowed down when it hits the floor, making it easier to catch, due to the backspin created by following through with your thumbs down.

Use the chest pass primarily in the open court and on the perimeter.

The ball should be thrown from your chest to the receiver's chest. By stepping into the pass with your knees bent and following through with thumbs down and fingertips last to contact the ball, the backspin will make the pass easier to catch.

Get the ball as close as possible to the entry line.

Imagine a line (entry line) drawn from the basket up through the key to half court. When throwing the basketball into play, it is important to get the ball as close as possible to this imaginary line in order to allow the receiving player ample opportunity for a good shot and to prevent the defenders from intercepting the ball.

Fake a pass to confuse a defender.

Before passing the ball while under pressure, it is wise to fake a pass first and then change it up. For example, fake a bounce pass, but actually throw the pass overhead or pretend to through the ball to the right, but actually throw it to the left. This will open up a clear area for you to really throw the ball.

Feed the post.

Passing angles are important when feeding the post. Be sure that the passer, the post and the basket area all in line so that when the defender commits to a side, the passer can throw the ball to the receiver on the other side, who can then drive directly to the basket.

Pass to the right player at the right time.

By focusing on who is open under the basket, you will become a better player and passer. As your peripheral vision improves, you will see who is open to pass the ball to without telegraphing your moves.

Improve your passing skill.

Passing is a very important aspect of basketball. Eye contact, crisp two-handed pass motion and follow through with thumbs pointing in the direction of the ball after it is thrown are key to passing. Passing to the target, meaning lead the player with the ball if necessary.

Take note of your defender's height.

Think of the best way to prevent a defender from intercepting the ball. For example, pass around or under a taller player and over a shorter one.

Use the overhead pass on the perimeter as an outlet pass or to bring the ball into play from the sidelines.

The ball is held straight up over the head, but not behind the head, without bending the elbows. The passer extends a leg toward the receiver while delivering the pass with a snap of the wrists and without a spin on the ball.

Know the importance of passing.

Coaches usually conduct the 'pass the court' drill to enhance their players' passing ability. It is done by positioning a player at each end of the court, at the top of each key and at mid-court. He then has them pass the ball from one end of the court to the other using eight passes. Meanwhile, he gets the best dribbler to try to beat them from one end of the court to the other. Unless the passing team messes up their passing, they will always beat the dribbler. This will instill the importance of passing.

Want to learn all these tips while actually doing them?

Visit
www.ArmChairGuides.com/PlayingBasketball

Sign up and download
your AUDIO COPY
of **Playing Basketball: An Arm Chair Guide Full of 100 Tips
to Getting Better at Basketball**
for FREE.

Need to multitask?
Need to relax your strained eyes after work?
Need to do your laundry?

Pick up some valuable advice to get you started and
integrate it into your lifestyle. Since the tips are being
read aloud, you'll no longer have a reason not to start
playing basketball.

Add more power.

When passing, always step into the pass. This will put more power behind your pass.

Know where the defense is.

Although knowing where your teammates are is important, knowing where the defense is even more important. You know where your teammates are through practice, peripheral vision and the identification of the uniforms. However, by concentrating on where the defense is, you can capitalize on their weak points and pass away from the defenders.

Use the two-handed bounce pass.

Holding the ball close to the chest with elbows in to the side of the body, the ball is released with a thrust of both arms and a snap of the wrists. Aiming for the receiver's thighs, the passer puts on foot forward and bounces the ball about ¾ of the way toward the receiver.

29

Confuse your defender.

The crossover is one of the more advanced basketball techniques and is used to confuse or get a jump on the opponent. Dribble at half to three-quarters of your full pace at the defender and then take a hard step to the side you are dribbling on and immediately bounce the ball across your body while accelerating to full speed with the opposite foot.

Practice the figure eights drill.

Players dribble the ball between their legs, forming the number eight (vertically). This drill is repeated until the player can perform at a rapid pace both forwards and backwards.

Improve agility, ball handling and defensive skills.

Coaches usually conduct the zigzag drill at practice in order to improve agility, ball handling and defensive skills. First, players dribble along the right side of the court at an angle. Once they get to the free-throw line, they cross over, dribbling with the other hand. This is repeated several times.

Use the high dribble for speed when there is a clear path to the basket.

The ball is bounced a little above the waist and slightly ahead of you. Do not use this dribble though when your opponents are near you since the ball might easily get stolen.

Try the low dribble for control.

The low dribble is used for control and to keep possession of the ball when the dribbler is closely guarded. It is more difficult for the defense to steal a low dribble than a high dribble. "Double-timing", which is speeding up the dribble while staying in place, helps to protect the ball and aids in faking out the opposition.

Change the pace of your dribble.

You can throw off opponents by changing up the speed of the dribble: from slow to fast and vice versa. You can drive around the opponent to the basket after getting him off stride.

Change your direction.

Using good footwork and ball handling, you can elude your opponent by changing the direction of the dribble from one hand to another. Make sure that your body is between the ball and your opponent.

Learn how to stop.

Stopping while dribbling can be tricky since a player can sometimes continue taking steps after stopping the dribble. This is called "traveling" and will give the opponent the ball. To prevent traveling, a player must keep the center of gravity low with knees low and one foot in front of the other, flat on the floor, and the rear foot slightly raised.

Push forward.

Always drive forward for a lay-up without hesitation. Knowing where to hit the backboard comes with a lot of practice.

Leap using one leg when doing a lay-up.

Leap using your stronger leg instead of stopping and jumping using both feet. Lead with your leg with your knee bent to propel yourself into the jump.

39

Use your arms.

When making a lay-up, add momentum after springing from your leg by swinging your arms upward with the ball towards the basket. Keep the ball in both hands until the peak of your jump and then transfer it to the performing hand.

Avoid driving to the hoop head-on.

Do not approach the basket head-on when attempting a lay-up since it is too hard to establish the correct depth perception. Make a lay-up from either side of the basket. Also focus on the basket the entire time instead of other players.

Practice on your own.

Practice on your own without other players present so that you can get your moves down without having to think about it. After spending a lot of time practicing, you can then practice against opponents.

Do a lay-up with your dominant hand.

Drive toward the basket while dribbling with your dominant hand. Take off close enough to the basket and make a lay-up. Recover the rebound and attempt another lay-up. See how many you can do in a row.

Lay up with your weaker hand.

Practice the previous drill, this time using your non-dominant hand. Lay up into the basket and make a rebound as many times as you can in a row. Take note of how many successful lay-ups you can do in a minute.

Alternate.

Do the same lay-up drill described previously, however, alternate using your dominant and non-dominant hands. Lay up into the hoop, grab the rebound, dribble back, then drive again towards the basket to make a lay-up. Repeat the steps and count the number of shots you've made.

45

Work on your jump stop.

A jump stop entails dribbling down the court and then landing on both feet at the same time while under control. After a jump stop, you can continue into a shot from any distance from the basket. A jump stop affords a strong base from which to shoot from. You can also pass the ball easily.

46

Practice your jump stops using objects placed around the court.

Dribble up to one of the objects and then jump stop. Make sure you are in control and do not travel. You must take off with one foot but land on both feet at the same time. You can either pass or shoot after your jump stop.

Make a V-cut.

By faking toward the rim and then sharply cutting back toward the ball, you can evade a defender. When viewed from above, this maneuver looks like a giant V. You change direction toward the ball once the defender turns his hips toward the ball.

Stay on the balls of your feet.

Quick pivots are fast cuts done on the balls of your feet. By playing on the balls on your feet, you can move more quickly while maintaining your balance.

49

Have the most physical balance.

You can maintain your balance by keeping your feet at least shoulder width apart. Bend slightly at the waist and knees while keeping your head mid-center. By maintaining this position you will be able to quickly respond to your opponent's movements.

Execute the L-cut.

Start at the bottom of the key and work your way up along its edge (walking your defender along) until you reach the top of the key. When your teammate is ready to pass you the ball, step into the defender, making slight contact, and then change speeds quickly away by pushing off of the inside foot to pop out to the wing.

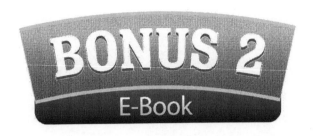

Bring these tips anywhere you go—
on the bus, train or while standing in line!

Head to
www.ArmChairGuides.com/PlayingBasketball

Sign up and grab
the **Playing Basketball: An Arm Chair Guide**
Full of 100 Tips to Getting Better at Basketball
E-BOOK BUNDLE (in PDF, ePub and Mobi) for FREE.

Do you want to read your Arm Chair Guides book on your device? Do you want to adjust the font size and still be able to add notes and bookmarks or highlight the text?

Download the free e-book bundle, which comes in 3 popular formats, and view them using your favorite reader. Learn some valuable tips to prepare for the game anytime, anywhere.

51

Learn how to pivot.

Pivoting is one of the important skills needed to get relief from defensive pressure. You turn on the ball of your foot to pivot; however, if your foot moves without dribbling, passing or shooting (including airborne shots), you are guilty of traveling and the ball is awarded to the other team. You can reverse pivot (turning backwards) or forward pivot (turning forwards).

Avoid traveling.

Once you have received the ball, you must not move from your established pivot foot until you pass, shot or dribble, otherwise you are traveling. "Positive footwork" is the term used to describe your "free" foot, which should be slightly forward of your pivot foot. This puts the player in charge rather than allowing the defender to "belly up" to the ball handler, making him retreat from the basket.

Balance during a pivot.

It is essential to maintain your balance during pivoting since extra steps will be called as traveling. Keep the ball at waist level and away from your opponent.

54

Try the drop step.

The drop step will force your opponent to go behind you, enabling you to take a clear shot when in the post. If you are at the bottom of the key and your opponent is closer to the free throw line, make your foot closest to the foul line your pivot foot. Take a strong step with the opposite foot directly toward the basket and take a shot.

Pivot firmly.

When making a pivot, do it firmly. Do not take several small pivot steps when one will work more to your advantage. Taking quick firm pivots will force your opponent off guard.

Choose the pivot foot.

Once you have established a pivot foot, you cannot change it until you pass, shoot or dribble. Wisely choose which foot would work better as the pivot foot before you take a step.

Use a jab step to drive or shoot.

Take a quick short step right at the defender while at the same time faking a dribble by bringing the ball down outside your knee. Pause for a split second and read the defender. If he comes toward you, you just extend the jab step to a longer step and push the ball out driving right off his hip. If the defender backs off on the jab step you pull back your lead foot and take the jump shot.

Set up by faking.

A screen is a player that places himself between their ball handler and the defensive player. The "screen" must be set before the ball handler moves otherwise he will be called for an offensive foul.

Faking before you set a screen will set the defensive player off balance and perhaps gain some time and distance between that player and the ball handler. Even a head fake can get the defender going the wrong direction or bumping into the screen.

Run shoulder-to-shoulder.

It is important for the ball handler to run shoulder-to-shoulder off of the screen. The defensive player cannot get around the screen and can either trail behind or commit a defensive foul.

"Explode" off of the screen so that the defensive player will be left behind.

This will also give the ball handler more time for a shot.

Make a good cut.

An effective cut is perfectly timed to arrive just in time to receive a pass. Making a slow good fake before a fast cut will gain you time and distance.

Do not avoid a defender when setting up a cut. Instead, "bounce off" of the defender so that he cannot react fast enough to cover your move. Slip out of sight of the defender by going behind him since the defender is concentrating on the ball.

Learn how to fake and sell it.

Fakes (shots or passes) are an important part of the game. If done properly, it will gain you some time and distance (even just one step on the defense) in order to receive a pass or take a shot.

Faking is not taught often enough. Even "looking" (look one way and throw another) a defender will keep the defense off-balance. You can fake with a look, your eyes, a head bob, a jab step, a shoulder roll, a "sleep fake" (pretending you are tired and bend over with your hands on your knees) or verbally by calling out a teammate's name.

Contest every shot your opponent makes.

At least put a hand up into the air so as to block the shooter's view or force him to shoot over you. Do not leave your feet until the shooter does and place your hand over the top of the ball to block it so that you do not commit a foul.

64

Form the defensive triangle.

Always anticipate the pass and position yourself so that you can interfere and deny the pass by placing your hands in the potential path of the ball. Position yourself between the ball and the player you are defending (unless he has the ball already). Use your peripheral vision to keep track of your opponent and the ball.

Move toward the ball.

Players should move as a team toward the ball (cover down) and yet keep track of the opponent players, especially their man (if playing man-to-man coverage). The player nearest the ball should cover that player. By clogging up the passing lanes, the ball can be forced out from the basket.

Position yourself between your opponent and the ball.

It is important to keep your body between your man and the basket while on defense within an arm's length so that you can pressure him. You will not be faked out by eye, head or shoulder fakes if you focus on your opponent's midsection. Also force him to go where he does not want to go by blocking his path to the basket.

Force the offense left or right.

By positioning yourself one foot to the left (or right) and one foot forward of your defensive stance, you can force the offense in the opposite direction. You want to position yourself to the right of left-handed players.

Keep a low stance.

A low stance with feet shoulder width apart, knees bent, butt down and back straight will position your nose to your opponent's chest. You should also keep your hands outside of your knees with palms up. In this way, you can change direction quickly which is essential for a good defense.

Do not let your defender pressure you into backing up.

Deny any defender that is posting you (with his back to the basket) access to the ball by placing yourself between him and the ball. Any contact with his elbows on your chest should be a foul against him.

Cover your man as he slides down the lane.

Place yourself between him and the ball thereby denying him the pass. Follow his lead with your hands in the air so that the ball handler will not pass to him since you can intercept the ball from this position.

Slide your feet.

The proper footwork for guarding a dribbler is to slide your feet instead of stepping, moving sideways as you place one foot shoulder width away and then place the other foot next to it before advancing the first foot to the side again. Always keep your feet in contact with the floor, making quick slides, staying low and keeping your feet wide apart when in motion.

Outlet the ball.

Once you gain possession of the ball, you stop playing defense and switch to offensive play. After the ball is shot, all five players move around the basket in a triangular shape in order to recover the rebound. After rebounding, the team can burst into a primary or secondary break for their basket.

Be in the proper position to receive a pass.

You must be in the proper position to receive a pass. This means you must "jump" to the ball or move forward to accept the ball. This allows you to not only receive the ball free from any interference, but this enables you to feed cutters or to aid your teammate in the event he is trapped with the ball.

74

Help and recover quickly when screening.

Not only are you responsible for the area you are "assigned" according to position, but you must step up and help your teammates. When your teammates steers the ball handler toward you, step up quickly. When the ball leaves your area, step back into position (recovery).

Learn to communicate with your teammates.

One quality of any great defensive team is the ability to communicate to one another quickly and clearly. By communicating by with verbal cues or through body language, you can stop the advancement of the ball of your opponent. This will make it difficult for the team to score against you.

Get the Tip of the Week delivered straight to your inbox!

Head to
www.ArmChairGuides.com/PlayingBasketball

Sign up
for the **Playing Basketball: An Arm Chair Guide
Full of 100 Tips to Getting Better at Basketball**
NEWSLETTER.

Join the Arm Chair Guides Newsletter and get a quick
basketball tip each week for one whole year.

Pressure the ball handler.

The key to being a good defender is to always put pressure on the ball handler. Don't let an offensive player do anything with the ball--dribble, pass, or shoot-- without having one of your hands trying to get in the way of the ball's path or his view of his teammates.

77

Deny the pass in from the side when guarding the high post (post player at the free throw line).

Deny the pass into the post with the forward arm while maintaining contact with your man with the back of your other hand. Once the ball is in play, get between your man and the basket.

Play weak-side or help defense when your man is two passes away from the ball.

If one of your teammate's men beats him, you must step up to block the drive. Be sure both feet are flat on the ground so that you do not draw a foul. Once you have stopped the drive, continue guarding your man with one hand pointing to the ball and the other hand on your man. Watch the ball and your man.

79

Use the close-out strategy.

When coming up to defend a player from a distance, sprint half way to him and then assume a low defensive position. Use shuffle steps to back up to the basket.

Get into position.

If a low post defensive player pushes you out of the best position, release and spin around him so that you position yourself between him and the basket 12 to 15 feet away from the basket. This makes it tough for the offense to shoot and easier for you to make a rebound.

81

Steal the ball.

Stealing or taking the ball away from an offensive player requires quick hands, timing and footwork in order not to foul. A skilled ball handler will always defend the ball from the defense. However, opportunities for stealing the ball present themselves and with experience, you will be ready.

Learn to block shots properly.

Blocking shots takes timing since you must touch the ball after it is released by the offensive player. A clean block is hitting the ball and not the shooters hand or arm. Big waving blocks will generally lead to a foul. After successfully blocking a shot, a player should capture the ball in order to score.

83

Position yourself between the basket and the post player.

This will be a constant struggle so be careful not to contact him to draw a foul. Lob passes will be the responsibility of your teammates since your focus is preventing the post player from receiving the ball in the key.

Double-team.

Whenever a low post player receives the ball, the outside player should quickly double-team him. This will make it difficult to take a shot, forcing the ball back outside.

85

Play a zone defense.

A zone defense is used when opponents can not successfully defend against it, man-to-man coverage is not possible, there is a need to control an excellent penetrating guard, or to sandwich the post player. Sometimes you can alternate between zone defense and man-to-man coverage.

Dictate the offense's direction.

Dictating the direction of the offense is invaluable. Simply place your right foot one foot to the right of the defensive player to force them to go right. Conversely, using your left foot will force them left. Practice with a teammate until you have this down. This can be used to direct an offensive player away from the basket.

87

Keep players out of the lane.

Coaches usually use this drill to teach players how to front and keep their opponents out of the lane. Start with the offense at the foul line with defensive players inside the lane facing them. The object is for the offense to try to pass the defense by blocking them with their arms and body. The defense can push the offense back with their hands on the upper arms and shoulders of the defense if the offense tries to charge the lane. This drill should be repeated six times for eight seconds each.

Assume that each shot is a miss.

Assuming that every shot is a miss will make you a good rebounder, offensively or defensively. You will always go after each shot and get ready to rebound if you think this way.

Pass to the guard for a fast break after a rebound.

By rebounding the ball quickly, pivoting away from the defense and outletting the ball to your guard, you can start a fast break for a score. This is extremely valuable to the team.

Try to go after each one.

You have to WANT the ball to be a good rebounder. Lean back on your man to keep him out of rebounding position. You do not have to be tall to be a good rebounder. Shorter players use footwork and body position to out-rebound taller players.

91

Get better at boxing out your opponent.

Box your opponent out of a good rebounding position by creating space from which to rebound. Pivot so your "butt is to your opponent's gut", sliding with him to keep him away from the rebound. Do not allow him to push you under the basket. Release from this position at the last moment in order to gain position.

92

Practice your "box out" moves.

Attitude and desire have as much to do with being a good rebounder as athletic ability. Practice your "box out" moves and you will become a valuable asset to your team.

93

Keep your hands up.

Your hands should always be up at least shoulder-high when getting ready to rebound. Remember, the ball will come off of the rim quickly and low. So when the shot goes up, your hands should too.

Take note of your position.

Concentration on the ball is as important as positioning in rebounding. Focus on the ball until it has been rebounded. Remember most shots rebound opposite to the side from which they were shot.

95

Strive to make an offensive rebound.

Since the defensive player has a "head start" in securing a good rebound position because he is already nearer to the basket, you must practice outmaneuvering him for position. Quickly changing directions, spinning or sweeping your leg in front of him can help. Offensive rebounding can get you some points since it is like a second chance at shooting at the basket.

Aim to make the perfect rebound.

A perfect rebound results from every player of a team boxing out their opponent so well that the rebound is easily caught AFTER it hits the floor. Practice is key in perfecting this maneuver.

Strengthen your ankles.

Ankle sprains are common in basketball. In order to combat this, try strengthening exercises lasting several minutes a day: walk on the outside of your feet, walk on the inside of your feet, walk on your toes and then finally, walk on your heels.

98

Warm up.

Warm-up is important since it allows your muscles to get ready for strenuous exercise. This decreases the chances of injury. You should be sweating before starting practice.

99

Stretch properly.

Since basketball requires flexibility, it is important to stretch out all of your muscles before a workout (and after, if you are weight training). Stretch to the point of resistance and hold for at least three seconds before repeating. Do not bob or rock since this can cause injury.

100

Make sure you've recovered fully before playing again.

It is important to completely heal from an injury before attempting to come back to play. Missing a preseason game is obviously smarter since you can then play for the rest of the season. Only play when there is no risk of further injury. A trainer and/or physician will determine the best time for you to return from an injury.

Conclusion

Basketball is a sport that's fun to watch yet even better to play. It helps develop teamwork and self-discipline, and at the same time keeps you in shape.

In order to succeed as a basketball player, you must perfect your skills, be confident and have the drive to improve. Practice will help hone your skills, but by playing often and against tough opponents, you will enhance your skills, confidence and drive. Are you ready for some basketball?

About Arm Chair Guides

Arm Chair Guides is a leading publisher of easy-to-read instructional and reference guides intended to help hobbyists just like us develop a better understanding of our passion through a series of short tips and advice.

Collected from across the globe via leading experts and topic authorities, each title consists of 100 tips focused on easily *implementable* ideas and techniques to help the hobbyist get the most from their pastime activities.

The perfect Christmas stocking stuffer, thank-you gift or *bedsider*, each Arm Chair Guide is designed to be a quick reference book that the reader can just pick up and flip through at their leisure.

To learn more about us and purchase our other titles, visit:
www.ArmChairGuides.com

Made in the USA
Lexington, KY
25 June 2011